Parade Of The Tin Soldiers

Primo

Graceful marching tempo

Primo

59

Duet from "Don Giovanni"
("La ci darem la mano")

Wolfgang A. Mozart

Moderately **Primo**

Scherzo (Duet)

PRIMO

Anton DIABELLI
(1781–1858)

The Waterman/Harewood Piano Series

Piano Progress Book 2

first classics – solo and duet

selected and edited by
Fanny Waterman and Marion Harewood

Faber Music Limited
London

Minuet in C minor

George Frederick Handel
(1685-1759)

Minuet

from The Little Notebook for Anna Magdalena Bach

Johann Sebastian Bach
(1685-1750)

Minuet

Wilhelm Friedemann Bach
(1710-1784)

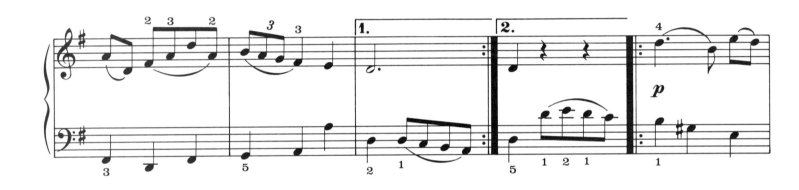

Minuet

Johann Christoph Bach
(1732-1795)

Ecossaise

from Op. 38

J. W. Hässler
(1747-1822)

Fanfare

William Duncombe
(18th century)

Canzonet

Christian Gottlob Neefe
(1748-1798)

Allegro

(K.1c)

(Salzburg. 11 December. 1761)

Wolfgang Amadeus Mozart
(1756-1791)

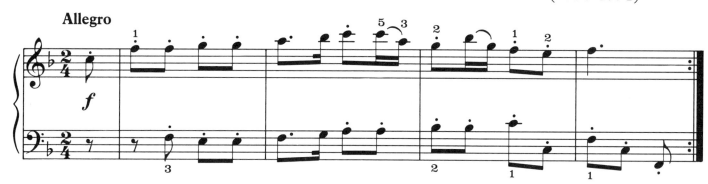

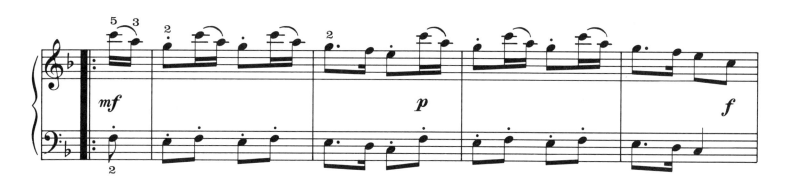

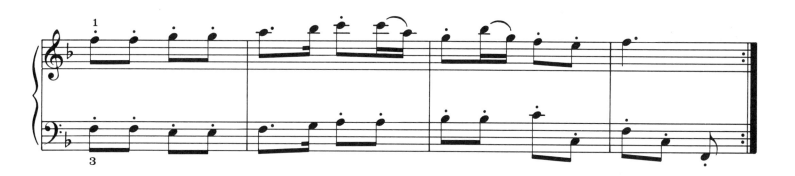

"A Slice of Bread and Butter"

Adapted from A Musical Trick

Wolfgang Amadeus Mozart
(1756-1791)

Tempo di Valse

★ Ascending *glissandi* are played with 2nd or 3rd finger, descending *glissandi* with thumb.
  Easier version: substitute scales for *glissandi*. - alter fingering accordingly.

Sad Memory

Daniel Steibelt
(1765-1823)

German Dance

Ludwig van Beethoven
(1770-1827)

Ballett

Carl Maria von Weber
(1786-1826)

Bear Dance

Robert Schumann
(1810-1856)

This piece appears on the flyleaf of Schumann's manuscript of "Album for The Young" Op. 60.

Hunting Horns

Theodor Oesten
(1813-1870)

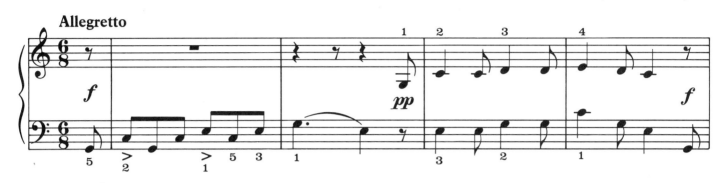

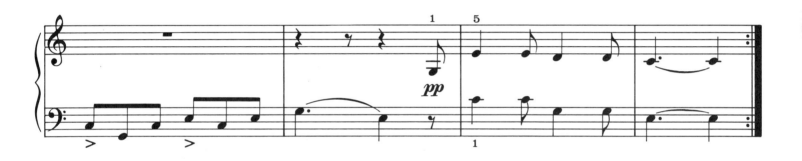

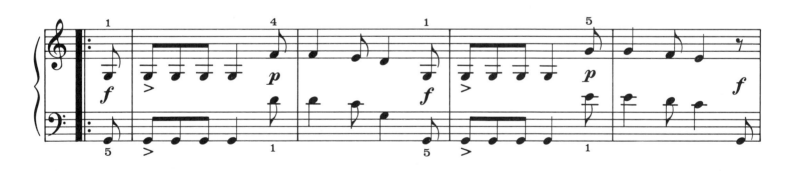

Lullaby

César Franck
(1822-1890)

Song

Op. 183 No. 1 from Serenade I

Carl Reinecke
(1824-1910)

Spanish Serenade

José Ferrer
(1835-1916)

Armenian Folk Dance

E. Hosrovian

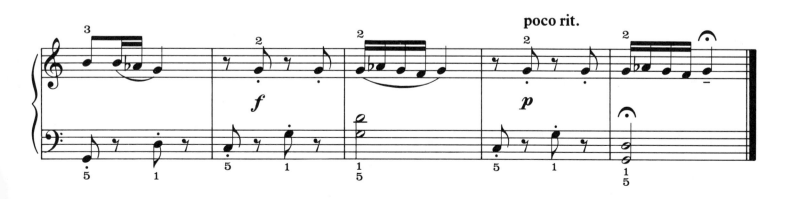

Swineherd's Dance

from " First Term at the Piano "

Béla Bartók
(1881-1945)

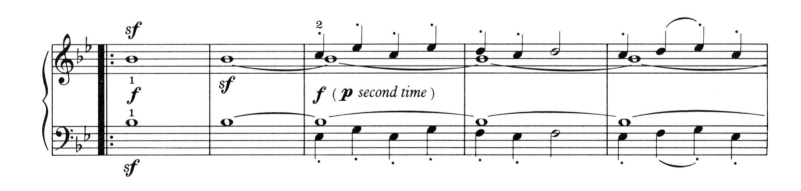

For the Kid Next Door

Soulima Stravinsky
(b. 1910)

The Hen

Secondo

J. E. Hummel

The Hen

Primo

J. E. Hummel
(19th century)

Turkish March

Secondo

Anton Diabelli

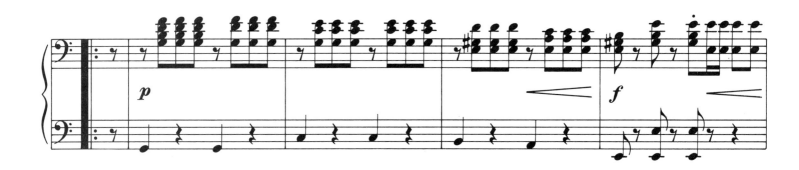

Turkish March

Primo

Anton Diabelli
(1781-1858)

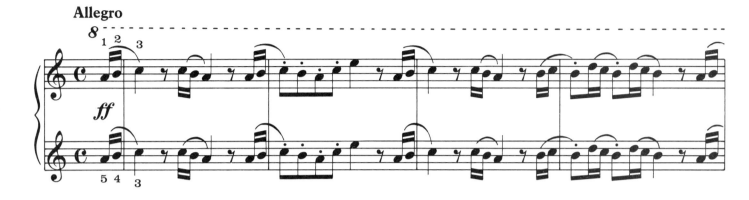

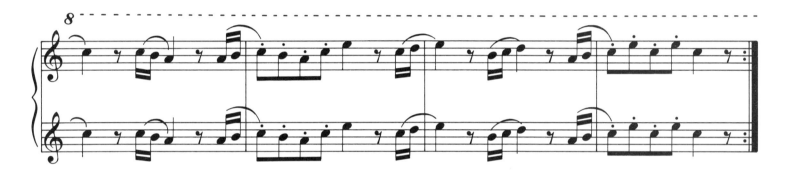

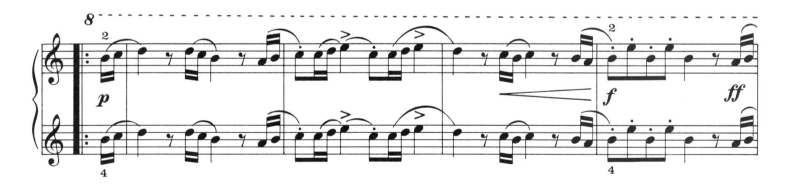

Sonatina

Secondo

Carl Maria von Weber

This is the first subject only of Weber's Sonatina in one movement.

Sonatina

Primo

Carl Maria von Weber
(1786-1826)

Rondino

Secondo

Anton Diabelli

Rondino

Primo

Anton Diabelli
(1781-1858)

Alabama Rag

Secondo

George Barnard

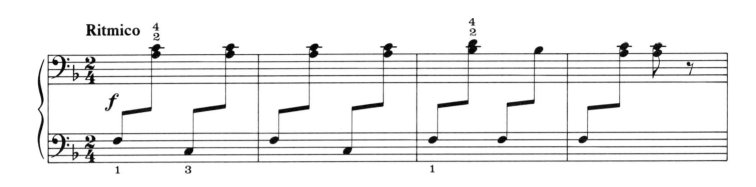

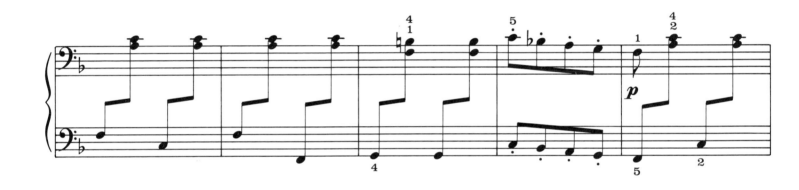

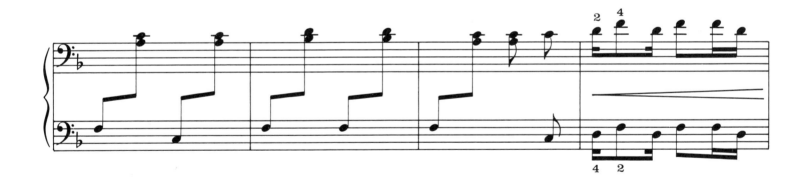

Alabama Rag

Primo

George Barnard
(fl. 1900)